EDWARD GOREY

THE AWDREY-GORE LEGACY

Pomegranate
San Francisco

Published by Pomegranate Communications, Inc.
Box 808022, Petaluma, CA 94975
800 227 1428   www.pomegranate.com

Pomegranate Europe Ltd.
Unit 1, Heathcote Business Centre, Hurlbutt Road
Warwick, Warwickshire CV34 6TD, UK
[+44] 0 1926 430111   sales@pomeurope.co.uk

This edition first published by Pomegranate Communications, Inc., 2010.

Library of Congress Control Number: 2010921493
ISBN 978-0-7649-5509-9

Pomegranate Catalog No. A187

Printed in China

19 18 17 16 15 14 13 12 11 10   10 9 8 7 6 5 4 3 2 1

For Agatha Christie

On last St Spasmus's day Miss D. Awdrey-Gore
was found dead at the age of 97. Just before
dawn a nameless poacher came upon her body
in a disused fountain on the estate of Lord
Ravelflap; she was seated bolt upright on a
gilt ballroom chair, one of a set of seventeen
then on display at Suthick & Upter's Auction
Rooms in Market Footling; her left hand
clutched a painted tin lily of cottage manufacture,
inside which was rolled up a Cad's Relish label
of a design superseded in 1947; something
illegible was pencilled on the back. That she
had been murdered was obvious, though as yet
the cause of death has not been determined.

It will be remembered that Miss Awdrey-Gore was one of the most prolific (*vide* our Two-Shilling Reprint Library) and celebrated writers of detective stories at the time of her unexpected disappearance on St Spasmus's eve in 1927. On various occasions since then, she has been reported (among a number of other possibilities) in a private lunatic asylum, living in Taormina dressed as a man, married to a Salubrian nobleman in Slobgut, or alternately, a garage mechanic in Idle-on-Sea, in religious retreat on the slopes of Kanchenjunga. But always falsely: her whereabouts for the past forty-four years remain unknown.

One moment she was sitting there;
The next, she'd vanished into air.
THE IPSIAD, *can. VI*

Several days after her reappearance, in a nearby suburban villa an oiled-silk packet came to light beneath the false bottom of an elephant's foot umbrella stand. Done up with mauve string and indigo blue sealing wax, it was addressed to my late grandfather, G. E. Deadworry, then (in 1927) head of Deadworry and Silt, her publishers. The packet's contents in their entirety— though certain things are patently missing— are reproduced on the following pages.

Roy Grewdead   Hon./Sir
Roger Addyew   Predilection for parsnips/
Drew Dogyear   cabbage
Grey Redwoad   Cribbage addict
Dedge Yarrow   Collects ticket stubs:
Orde Graydew   covering screen

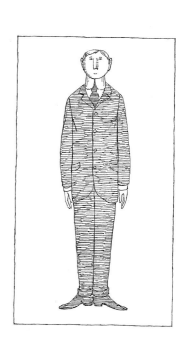

> To catch and keep the public's gaze
> One must have lots of little ways.
> THE IPSIAD, *can. IV*

Waredo Dyrge
Half Irish, half Japanese
Has been soldier of fortune and progressive
   victim of explosions all over the world
Now England's most sought-after private
   detective
Has possibly world's most valuable collection
   of artificial hands, many of them given to
   him by grateful clients
Will never take up a case on a Tuesday

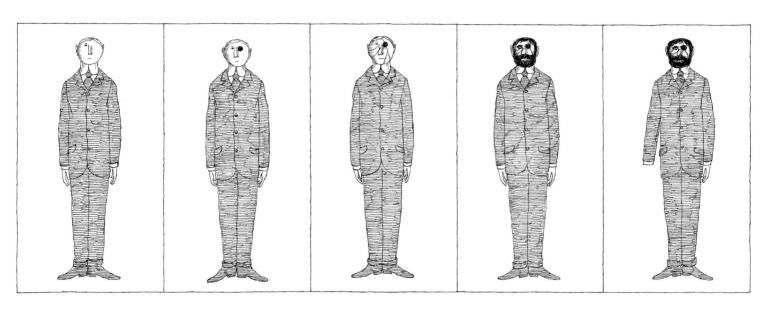

His deductions concerning each case are
given in the form of a linked series of haiku
in Gaelic of his own composition; each is
presented to the reader as it is made in a
literal English translation that, while strange
and vague in the extreme, turns out to
have been perfectly fair and even obvious.

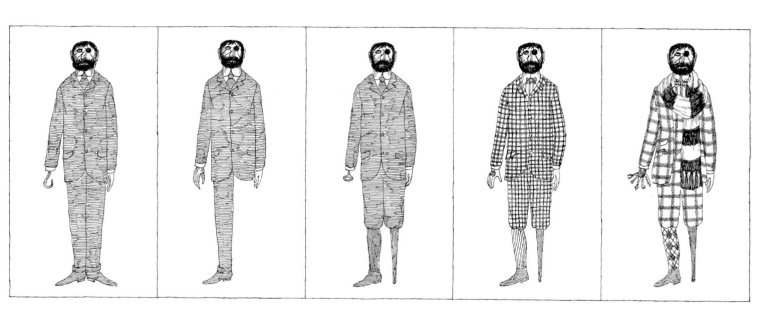

Deary, his inseparable and ferocious companion, is named for his master's favourite reading – the Deary Rewdgo Series for Intrepid Young Ladies (*D.R. on the Great Divide, D.R. in the Yukon, D.R. at Baffin Bay,* etc.) by Dewda Yorger. He is familiar with thirty-seven different hand signals, and has a passionate fondness for Cad's Relish on water biscuits.

Of all the people on the scene
Some are betwixt and some
between.
THE IPSIAD, *can. II*

Heroine (if she turns out to be the murderer, have a second with different hair colour)

Amateur cricketer/sailor/explorer Architect
Heir to title and/or estate Childhood friend

Owner of great estate   Local magistrate
Baronet   M.F.H.   Member of Parliament

County/not quite county lady   Owner of fabulous
jewels   Hostess of weekend house party

Curate/Vicar/Dean/Bishop   Escaped lunatic
Cousin from Tasmania

Real/bogus Middle European nobleman
Gigolo   Secret agent for us/them

Author of standard work on string figures   Indigent
cousin Axe murderess in forgotten *cause célèbre*

Member of the upper class gone to the bad
Lower class person with a grudge

Unsuccessful poet Successful interior decor-ator Unsuitable friend of heroine/hero

Lady novelist Lady with passion for flowers/dogs / other ladies Scottish cousin

Duke / Dowager duchess Village ancient Superannuated governess/gardener

Postmistress Housekeeper Seamstress
Companion Cousin who is retired missionary

American millionaire Newspaper proprietor
Prime minister Condiment tycoon

Famous/notorious actress Unsuitable friend of
hero/heroine Cousin living at Antibes

Doctor Solicitor Secretary Friend of family Spy
Jewel thief Cousin who inherits everything

Provincial music-hall star Owner of fashionable
supper club Nurse Cousin by marriage

The authorities : local / Scotland Yard

It's most unlikely that his bed
Is where the victim's lying dead.
THE IPSIAD, *can.III*

Ha-ha

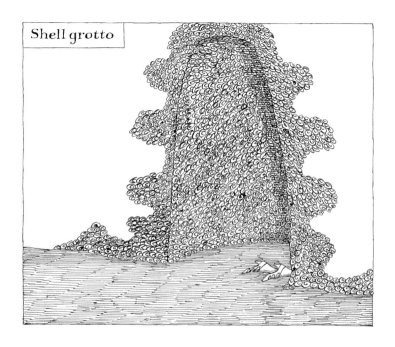

Shell grotto

Library

Standing stone

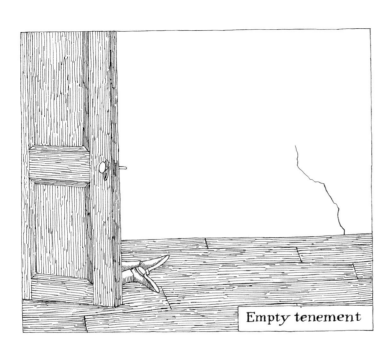

Empty tenement

Dinghy

He was, it's said, somehow done in
With nothing but a safety pin.
THE IPSIAD, *can. VI*

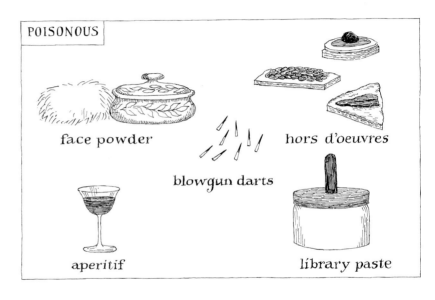

POISONOUS

face powder

blowgun darts

hors d'oeuvres

aperitif

library paste

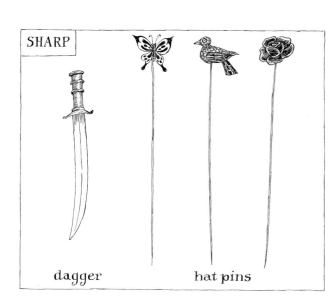

SHARP

dagger   hat pins

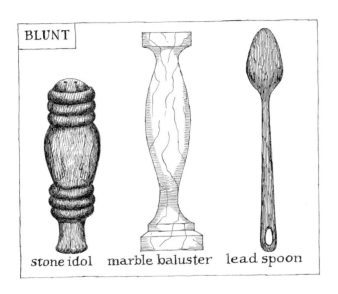

stone idol   marble baluster   lead spoon

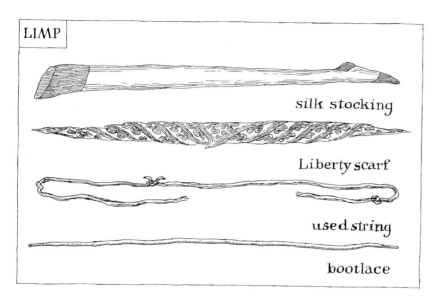

LIMP

silk stocking

Liberty scarf

used string

bootlace

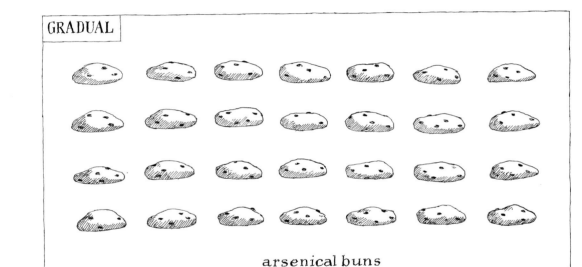

GRADUAL

arsenical buns

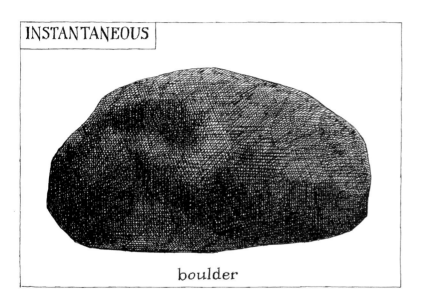

boulder

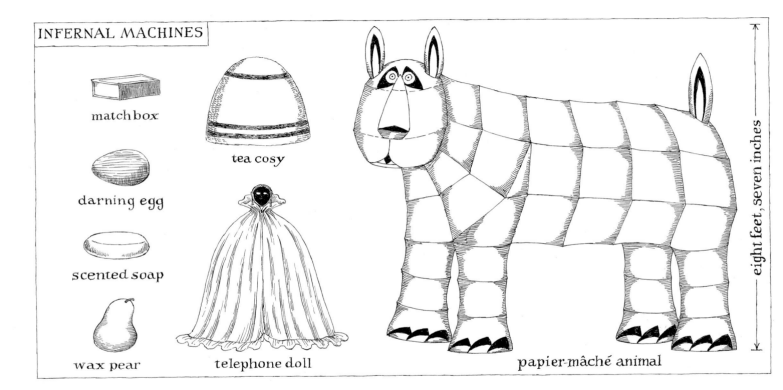

INFERNAL MACHINES

match box

darning egg

scented soap

wax pear

tea cosy

telephone doll

papier-mâché animal

eight feet, seven inches

INEXPLICABLE

confetti

The crucial information can
Be hidden in a simple plan.
THE IPSIAD, *can. VIII*

Cross section of fountain from west showing faulty pipe

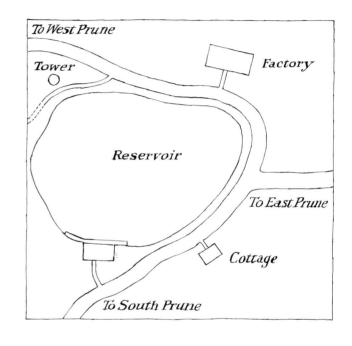

The labyrinth at 3:27 after Miss Gentian had
successfully found her way in and back

The labyrinth at 4:09 when Harold Tyne-
Forque gave up trying to reach its heart.

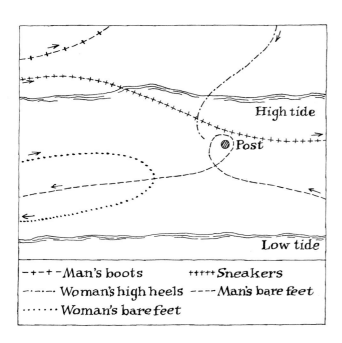

High tide

Post

Low tide

-+-+- Man's boots ++++ Sneakers

-·-·- Woman's high heels ---- Man's bare feet

····· Woman's bare feet

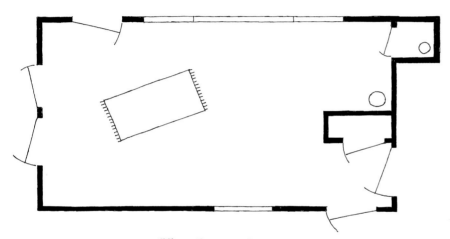

The Celery Room
Showing position of vases and rug

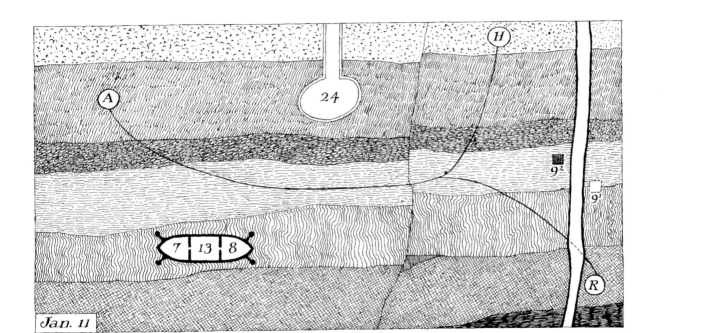

The smallest clue may be (or not)
The one to give away the plot.
THE IPSIAD, *can. I*

ᛋᚾᚻᛒᛒᛁᛏᛌ ᛚᛁᛋᛏ
ᛁᚦᚦᛋ
ᛒᚢᛏᛏᚱ
ᛁᛉᛏᛚᛋ
ᛁᛏᚠᛋ ᚱᛁᚾᛚᛉ
ᛏᚢᚱᛏᛁᛒᛋ
ᛏᛁᛏ
ᛋᛉᛏᛒ

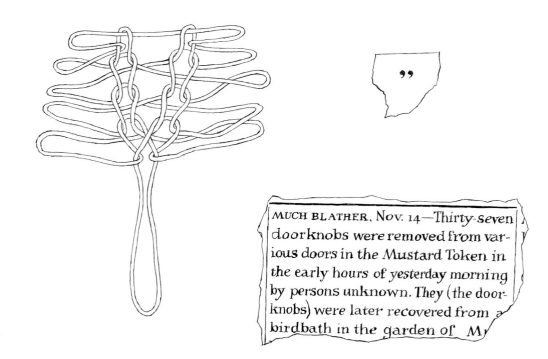

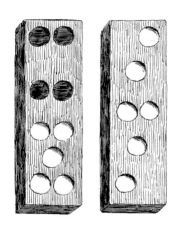

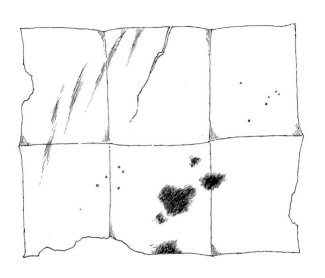

Nᵒ 7046

P.T.O.

> Perhaps *it* might be even subtler
> If after all it *was* the butler.
> THE IPSIAD, *can. IX*

Isla Trope is really _Lord Onion_ 's _great granddaughter_

At _11.17 the door to the winter garden_ was _already locked and bolted_

James Grumesdaul and _Charles Toast_ are really the same person

George Utmost is really not _Daphne Soot_ 's _cousin from Wyoming_

On the _14th_ of _January_ the '_Larko Sandargo_' was _still off the coast of Iceland_

Lady Truss is really two entirely different people

What the murderer failed
to realize is that
there is no Number
Fourteen, Bandage
Terrace

What the murderer failed
to realize is that
yellow stitchbane
is not yellow at all,
but a pale mauve

What the murderer failed
to realize is that
the Great Northwest
Road does not go
beyond Little Remorse

What the murderer failed
to realize is that
Grumblotch's salts
are not soluble in
lemonade

What the murderer failed
to realize is that
at high tide the outermost
of Saint Loola's Rocks
is completely submerged

The guilty found, there's little wait
Before they're overcome by fate.
THE IPSIAD, *can. XIII*

Cyanide pill

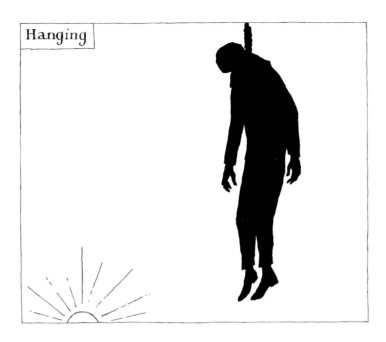

Madness

Over the cliff

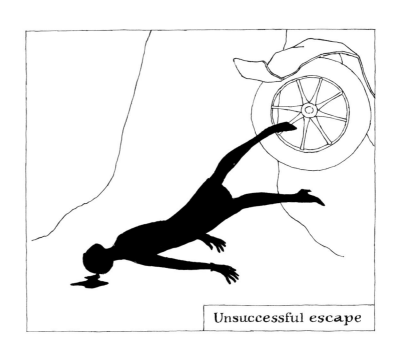

Unsuccessful escape

Successful escape

And what if then we don't find out
What all of it has been about ?

THE IPSIAD, *can.XI*

The Great ███ ern Road

Lily thinks she left
her eau-de-Nil scarf
under the cushions
on the chaise-longue
in the lounge.
Trebonianus Gallus
bit Mr. Trapbat
again. Higs.

These postcards recently fell out of a discarded lending-library copy of *The Teacosy Crime*, perhaps Miss Awdrey-Gore's most popular work. It will be noticed they were never sent, or, for that matter, even addressed.

No. ▆, ▆▆▆ Terrace, ▆▆chester

Post card Carte postale Postkarte Cartolina postale
Dopisnice Открытое письмо Levelező-Lap Briefkaart.

Send at once
recipe for
plaice with
thyme.

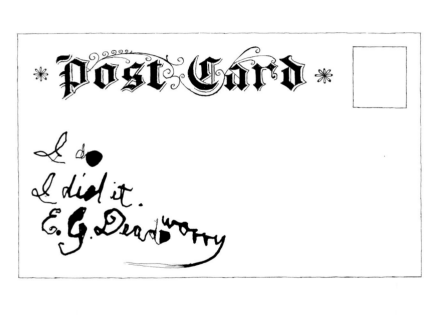

Edward Gorey books by Pomegranate, in print or coming soon:

The Black Doll: A Silent Screenplay by Edward Gorey
The Blue Aspic
Category
The Dong with a Luminous Nose, text by Edward Lear
The Eclectic Abecedarium
Edward Gorey: Three Classic Children's Stories
Edward Gorey: The New Poster Book
Elegant Enigmas: The Art of Edward Gorey
Elephant House: or, the Home of Edward Gorey, by Kevin McDermott
The Gilded Bat
The Hapless Child
The Jumblies, text by Edward Lear
The Remembered Visit
The Sopping Thursday
The Twelve Terrors of Christmas, text by John Updike
The Utter Zoo
The Wuggly Ump

. . . and don't miss
The Fantod Pack
Edward Gorey's Dracula: A Toy Theatre